LEAD THE LIGHT WAY™
PARENT EDITION

Raising Children with Love, Integrity, Goodness,
Humility & Transparency

Beverly K. Girton

DEDICATION

To every parent doing the best they can, even on the days it feels like too much.

To the mothers and fathers learning as they go, growing while they guide, and leading even when they don't feel ready.

And to my own children—now adults—who taught me as much as I taught them,

and to my grandchildren, who call me **"Grandma Cookie"**, and light my heart in ways words cannot explain.

This book is for you.

May you lead the LIGHT Way, one day and one moment at a time.

— Beverly

TABLE OF CONTENTS

PREFACE

Why LIGHT Matters in the Home

There is no place where leadership is more needed—or more often overlooked—than inside the home. Many parents feel overwhelmed, stretched thin, or unsure of themselves. They want to protect, support, guide, and nurture their children… but they don't always feel equipped.

For years, I have taught the LIGHT principles—**Love, Integrity, Goodness, Humility, Transparency**—in churches, nonprofits, classrooms, and corporate spaces. Everywhere I went, I heard the same words:

"This would help me as a parent."

"I need these principles with my kids."

"My home could use this clarity and peace."

The more I worked with leaders, the more I saw a truth we often forget:

Leadership at home is the foundation of leadership everywhere else.

If we want emotionally healthy adults, we must raise emotionally healthy children.

If we want strong communities, we must strengthen families first.

This book is not about perfect parenting.

It is about purposeful parenting.

It is an invitation to lead with LIGHT—

in your conversations, your corrections, your boundaries, your emotions, your expectations, and your daily interactions.

May this book become a companion to your parenting journey—a reminder that God entrusted you with influence, and that you have everything you need to guide your child with love and confidence.

FOREWORD

Foreword by Lilisa J. William

By Lilisa J. William, Leadership Coach & LIGHT Training

Partner Parenting is one of the most meaningful leadership roles any person will ever hold, and yet it is often the role we feel least prepared for. When Beverly first shared the LIGHT framework with me in 2014—during a thought leadership session I invited her to— I immediately recognized the significance of what she had created: a simple, powerful model rooted in Love, Integrity, Goodness, Humility, and Transparency. That original presentation sparked something deep. It was clear that LIGHT wasn't just a leadership tool for organizations—it was a life framework with the power to strengthen families, communities, ministries, workplaces, and hearts. Over the years, I've had the privilege of encouraging Beverly as she expanded LIGHT into a full leadership philosophy. And now, as we prepare to deliver training together—combining her Lead the LIGHT Way with my Release Your Power™ programs—I can see even more clearly how transformational this work truly is. This Parent Edition is one of the most important expressions of LIGHT, because home is the first classroom of leadership. Children learn how to love, listen, trust, and communicate by watching the adults around them. Beverly's guidance in these pages is both practical and soulful—helping parents lead with clarity rather than chaos, connection rather than conflict, and peace rather than pressure. If you are holding this book, you are choosing to lead your home with purpose and intention. May these pages encourage you, strengthen you, and remind you that LIGHT-led parenting is not about perfection—it's about presence, growth, and grace. Your home will shine brighter because of the LIGHT you carry.

— **Lilisa J. Williams**
Leadership Coach & LIGHT Training Partner

INTRODUCTION

The Heart Behind LIGHT-Led Parenting

Parenting is one of the most meaningful—and often one of the most challenging—roles a person can hold. Every day you are shaping a human soul: their confidence, their character, their coping skills, their understanding of love, and the way they respond to the world.

Most parents don't feel prepared, but you are not alone. The LIGHT principles—Love, Integrity, Goodness, Humility, and Transparency—help parents lead with clarity and confidence.

Welcome. This is the beginning of leading your home the LIGHT Way.

WHY I WROTE THIS PARENT EDITION

A Message From My Heart to Yours

Parents everywhere kept telling me: "I need this in my home." I realized the same leadership principles that strengthen churches and organizations also restore peace, connection, and clarity inside families.

I wrote this edition because home is the first place where children learn how to love, trust, communicate, handle conflict, and grow.

HOW TO USE THIS BOOK

A Simple Guide for Parents in Every Season

Read this book at your own pace. Pause at the Reflection Questions. Focus on one LIGHT principle at a time. Use the 30-Day LIGHT Parenting Journal as a reset space. Return to chapters as needed.

This is your companion, not a pressure-filled workbook.

WHAT YOU CAN EXPECT

A Journey of Grace, Growth, and Practical Tools

You will find practical guidance, emotional encouragement, and tools that strengthen your home. Expect clarity, compassion, and growth—not perfection. This book is designed to empower you, not overwhelm you.

NOTE TO PARENTS

Dear Parent,

I want you to know something before you begin this journey:

You are not behind.

You are not failing.

You are not alone.

This book is not here to judge your past choices or pressure you into perfection. It is here to help you lead with clarity, grow with grace, and create an emotionally healthy atmosphere for your child.

Read at your own pace.

Take what helps.

Give yourself permission to learn as you go.

Your presence matters.

Your growth matters.

Your leadership matters.

And your LIGHT will make a difference more than you can ever imagine.

With love,

Beverly

PART ONE

The LIGHT principles in the home

CHAPTER ONE

Parenting Is Leadership

Why Your Influence Matters More Than You Think

Parenting is one of the most sacred assignments God gives us. It stretches us, shapes us, humbles us, and grows us all at the same time. And yet, many parents don't see themselves as leaders. They see themselves as caregivers, helpers, supporters, protectors… but not leaders.

But here's the truth:

Every parent is a leader — whether they feel like one or not. Leadership is influence, and no one influences a child more than the people who raise them. You are shaping their worldview, their confidence, their habits, their ability to problem-solve, and the way they treat others. You are imprinting on their hearts what love feels like, what trust looks like, and how grace is lived out in real time.

You do this not by being perfect, but by being present.

Not by knowing everything, but by learning while you lead.

No corporate CEO makes more important decisions than a parent.

No ministry leader impacts more lives daily than a mother or father guiding a child.

No title is greater than the one your children use when they call for you.

Yet so many parents feel discouraged. They wonder if they're doing enough, saying enough, or modeling enough. They sometimes feel unseen, unheard, and undervalued. And they quietly question whether their influence is reaching their children at all.

If that's you… you are not alone. And you are not failing.

Leadership — especially parenting leadership — is rarely measured in the moment.

It is measured in memories, in values, in resilience, in character, in the long game of life.

And your children will carry your voice, your lessons, your LIGHT, long after they grow.

The Leader Your Child Doesn't Always See — But Always Feels

Children don't always respond with gratitude. They don't always obey quickly. They don't always understand the sacrifices you make. And when they grow into teens or young adults, they may take paths you wish they wouldn't.

But none of that cancels your leadership.

You are still the anchor.

Still the blueprint.

Still the emotional home they return to — even if they first wander through the world looking for their own answers.

Your children may take the long route, but your influence remains permanent.

Your LIGHT still shines in their spirit.

Your voice still sits in their heart.

Your prayers still surround their steps.

And while they are forming their own testimonies, your leadership is forming their foundation.

Why Parenting Requires LIGHT Leadership

In the Lead the LIGHT Way™ framework, leadership is built on five pillars:

- ❖ Love
- ❖ Integrity
- ❖ Goodness
- ❖ Humility
- ❖ Transparency

At home, these principles don't just guide your leadership —
they transform it.

- ❖ Love becomes your anchor.
- ❖ Integrity becomes your consistency.
- ❖ Goodness becomes your daily example.
- ❖ Humility becomes your safety zone.
- ❖ Transparency becomes your connection point.

These are not corporate skills.

These are not ministry skills.

These are human skills — skills that shape the emotional and
spiritual health of your home.

When LIGHT shows up in your parenting, your children feel
seen, heard, valued, corrected with grace, and led with
intention.

This is the leadership that builds emotionally secure
children.

REFLECTION: "A Leader at Home"

Take a moment to breathe and answer the questions below.
There is no judgment here — just awareness and grace.

1. Do I see myself as a leader in my home? Why or why
   not?

   Write your honest thoughts.

2. What messages did I receive about leadership growing up?

   How do those influence me today?

3. In what ways am I already leading my children well?

   List 3 strengths you bring to your parenting leadership.

4. What area do I want to grow in as a parent-leader this season?

   Choose one — not five.

You Don't Have to Lead Perfectly — Just LIGHT-ly

Perfection has never raised a healthy child.

Presence has.

Grace has.

Consistency has.

Honesty has.

Warm correction has.

Love — patient, listening, compassionate love — has.

Your child doesn't need a perfect parent.

They need a LIGHT parent.

Someone who tries.

Someone who apologizes.

Someone who models what growth looks like.

Someone who is willing to learn and lead at the same time.

Children follow what they see more than what they hear.

And when they see Love, Integrity, Goodness, Humility, and Transparency lived out daily, they don't just behave differently — they become different.

They become more confident.

More secure.

More resilient.

More kind.

More willing to trust, communicate, and tell the truth.

Because your LIGHT becomes their leadership training for life.

REFLECTION: "My Leadership Imprint"

1. What do I hope my child remembers about me when they look back on their childhood?
2. What emotions do I want my presence to create in my home?
5. Peace? Safety? Joy? Confidence? Belonging? Something else?
3. What is one small, simple action I can take this week to lead my home with more LIGHT?

The Beginning of a New Way of Parenting

This journey is not about being hard on yourself — it is about becoming more aware, more intentional, and more aligned with the parent you want to be.

You are not starting from scratch.

You are starting from experience.

You are starting from love.

You are starting from God's grace.

And you are stepping into leadership that has the power to transform your home for generations.

This is the beginning of LIGHT-led parenting.

A new way forward.

A gentler, stronger, more connected way.

A way that keeps you growing while you guide.

A way that allows your children to flourish while you lead without fear or guilt.

Welcome to the Parent Edition of the Lead the LIGHT Way™.

You were created for this.

And your children will benefit from the LIGHT you carry.

CHAPTER TWO

LOVE: Holding Care and Clarity Together at Home

The Heartbeat of LIGHT Parenting

Love is the foundation of every healthy home. It is the safety net, the anchor, the atmosphere, and the rhythm that shapes how children grow, feel, and connect.

But in parenting, love is more than affection or warm feelings. It is more than kisses on the forehead, bedtime stories, or making their favorite meal. Those are beautiful expressions of love—but they are not the full picture.

Love Also Looks Like Resilience in Real-Life Hardships

Love does not always look soft or sentimental.

Sometimes love looks like strength.

For many parents—especially those working long hours, raising large families, or navigating hardship—love is expressed through resilience.

Love looks like getting up early, coming home late, and still giving what you can.

Love looks like stretching resources, juggling schedules, and finding a way to meet each child's needs.

Love looks like steady presence, even when time and energy are limited.

Love looks like sensing which child needs comfort, which one needs guidance, and which one needs a moment with you.

This kind of love may not be glamorous, but it is powerful.

It is protective.

It is stabilizing.

It is leadership under pressure.

Some of us grew up with parents who showed love this way—through sacrifice, perseverance, and a quiet determination to keep the family together. Their love taught us strength, endurance, and loyalty. It wasn't always perfect, but it was always present.

Love is not just what you feel.

It is what you carry.

It is what you continue doing, even when life is heavy.

This too is LIGHT-led parenting.

Real love in parenting is care and clarity held together.

It is compassion with boundaries.

Patience with expectations.

Warmth with truth.

Grace with accountability.

Love is both gentle and guiding.

Comforting and correcting.

Soft and strong.

Too much softness without guidance creates confusion.

Too much firmness without warmth creates distance.

But love that holds both care and clarity creates children who feel safe, secure, supported, and guided.

This is the foundation of LIGHT-led parenting.

Love as Compassion, Patience, Respect (C.P.R.)

In the Lead the LIGHT Way™, love expresses itself through Compassion, Patience, Respect (CPR).

Compassion

Compassion helps you understand the "why" behind your child's behavior. It slows you down long enough to ask:

- ❖ What is their heart saying?
- ❖ What is the need beneath the behavior?
- ❖ Where is their frustration coming from?

Compassion doesn't excuse behavior, but it interprets it.

Respect

Respect in parenting means honoring your child's personality, their pace, their differences, and their feelings— even when those feelings are messy or loud or inconvenient. Respect says:

"I value who you are while I guide who you are becoming."

It means adjusting your approach when the way you naturally respond would overwhelm or shut them down.

Patience

Patience is not simply waiting.

It is how you wait.

Parenting requires spiritual patience—patience that allows room for growth, mistakes, learning curves, emotional development, and maturity.

Love that includes patience says:

"You don't have to get it right the first time.

We're learning together."

Compassion, Patience, Respect are not weaknesses.

They are leadership strengths.

Love Also Holds Clarity

Some parents lead with so much warmth that children feel loved but lack direction.

Others lead with so much structure that children have direction but lack connection.

Clarity is how you balance that tension.

Clarity in parenting means:

- ❖ clear expectations
- ❖ consistent boundaries
- ❖ predictable responses
- ❖ simple rules
- ❖ follow-through
- ❖ spoken values
- ❖ calm correction
- ❖ structure that children can count on

Clarity gives your child emotional security because it makes the world feel stable.

Children thrive when the rules are simple, the boundaries are consistent, and the consequences make sense.

Love gives children comfort.

Clarity gives them confidence.

When you put the two together, your home becomes a place where your child can grow without fear.

REFLECTION: "How Do I Show Love?"

1. In what ways do I naturally show love to my children?

   Affection? Gifts? Time? Words? Acts of service? Something else?

2. Where do I struggle to hold both care and clarity together?

    What tends to fall out of balance?

3. What part of CPR (Compassion, Patience, Respect) comes easiest for me?

    Which is hardest?

How Love Responds vs. Reacts

Reactions come from emotion.

Responses come from intention.

Every parent has moments of reacting—it's human. But LIGHT parents learn to pause long enough to shift from reacting to responding.

Responding looks like:

- ❖ lowering your tone
- ❖ stepping away for 10 seconds
- ❖ choosing kind words
- ❖ separating the child from the behavior
- ❖ remembering their age and development
- ❖ breathing before speaking
- ❖ asking questions before correcting

Responding requires self-management.

That is a form of love.

Reacting quickly often escalates a situation.

Responding intentionally often heals it.

Love is not the absence of frustration; it is the presence of restraint.

REFLECTION: "My Love Patterns"

1. When I feel overwhelmed, do I tend to react or respond? Why?

2. What one change could help me respond with more calm and clarity?

Love That Corrects Without Crushing

Children need correction.

They need guidance.

They need accountability.

They need boundaries that protect, not punish.

But they do not need shame.

They do not need fear.

They do not need emotional withdrawal.

They do not need silent treatment or harsh words.

Love corrects behaviors without crushing the child's spirit.

Love says:

❖ "You made a mistake, but you are still good."

❖ "This behavior needs correcting, but you are still loved."

❖ "You can try again."

Correction should never make a child question their worth.

It should guide their choices, not wound their identity.

Loving correction builds:

- ❖ resilience
- ❖ responsibility
- ❖ emotional safety
- ❖ trust
- ❖ confidence

This is the LIGHT way.

The Leadership of Love in Everyday Moments

Love is not loud.

It is expressed in repeatable, simple, daily moments:

- ❖ How you greet your child in the morning
- ❖ How you say goodnight
- ❖ The softness in your voice when they are upset
- ❖ The grace you give when they mess up
- ❖ The interest you show in their day
- ❖ The warmth you bring to routines
- ❖ The steadiness you offer during conflict

Love does not just show up in big family moments—it shows up in the ordinary.

Those are the moments children remember forever.

REFLECTION: "Love in My Daily Routine"

1. What simple daily interactions can I make more loving or intentional?
2. How do I want my child to experience my love this week?

A Final Word: Love Is Your Leadership Language

Children feel love through consistency, honesty, presence, tone, and touch.

They feel love through the boundaries that keep them secure.

They feel love through the time you make, the grace you extend, and the truth you speak.

Love is the greatest leadership language you speak at home.

And when your love includes compassion, patience, respect, and clarity, your home becomes a safe, nurturing place where your child can flourish emotionally, spiritually, and mentally.

This is not just parenting.

This is leadership.

This is transformation.

This is LIGHT.

CHAPTER THREE

INTEGRITY: Doing What's Right Even When It's Hard

The Quiet Strength Children Learn by Watching You

Integrity in parenting is not about being perfect.

It is about being principled.

It means being the same person in public and at home…

consistent in love, consistent in boundaries, and consistent in truth.

Children do not learn integrity because we tell them to "be honest," "be responsible," or "do the right thing."

They learn integrity because they see us choosing the right thing — even when the easy thing would be faster, quieter, or more convenient.

Integrity is lived more than taught.

It is caught more than instructed.

In a world full of shifting values and blurred lines, a parent's integrity becomes a child's anchor. It gives them a model for how to navigate pressure, temptation, disappointment, and mistakes.

And the most powerful part?

Children rarely say, "Thank you for teaching me integrity."

But they carry it into adulthood — and that is the thank-you.

Integrity When Life Is Tough

Parenting with integrity does not happen in ideal conditions.

It happens in real life — in the stress, in the pressure, in the long days and late nights.

Integrity is choosing what's right even when you're stretched thin.

Even when you're tired.

Even when you're carrying the weight of work, finances, responsibilities, or raising multiple children with different needs.

For many parents, life's demands make integrity feel harder…

but they also make integrity more meaningful.

Integrity in tough seasons looks like:

- ❖ trying again after a hard day
- ❖ calming your voice when your nerves feel worn
- ❖ telling the truth even when it complicates things
- ❖ apologizing even when you're exhausted

- ❖ following through even when it would be easier not to
- ❖ showing steadiness even when life around you feels unstable
- ❖ modeling resilience because you want your child to learn strength

This is the kind of integrity many of us grew up watching — especially in homes where parents had to work long hours or manage big families with limited resources.

Even when the world was heavy, they stayed grounded.

Even when circumstances were hard, they kept their word as best they could.

Even when life felt overwhelming, they tried again the next day.

That quiet, consistent effort?

Children remember it.

It becomes the integrity they carry into their adult lives.

Integrity is not about never being shaken.

It is about staying rooted even in the storm.

Integrity Is Consistency of Character

Integrity means your child knows what to expect from you.

Not perfection — predictability.

They know:

- ❖ your yes means yes

- ❖ your no means no
- ❖ your promises matter
- ❖ your boundaries remain
- ❖ your reactions don't shift with your mood
- ❖ your expectations don't change day to day

Consistency creates emotional safety.

Emotional safety creates trust.

Trust builds connection.

Connection gives you influence.

And influence — not control — is what real leadership is built on.

Integrity keeps a home steady.

REFLECTION: "Am I Consistent?"

1. What is one area where my follow-through is strong?

   (e.g., bedtime routines, consequences, affection, discipline, communication)

2. What is one area where I struggle with consistency?

   What makes it challenging?

3. How do my children respond when I follow through?

   How do they respond when I don't?

Integrity Is Doing What's Right — Even When No One Notices

Parenting integrity includes the "hidden moments":

- ❖ being truthful with your child even when it's uncomfortable
- ❖ apologizing when you're wrong
- ❖ keeping commitments they will remember
- ❖ treating them with respect even when you feel stretched thin
- ❖ showing self-control even when frustrated

Children watch how you treat:

- ❖ waiters
- ❖ teachers
- ❖ strangers
- ❖ family members
- ❖ people who frustrate you

Your behavior teaches them:

- ❖ how to respond to conflict
- ❖ how to tell the truth
- ❖ how to stand for what's right
- ❖ how to own mistakes
- ❖ how to handle pressure

Your integrity becomes their internal compass.

They are learning from what you model far more deeply than from what you say.

Integrity Also Means Keeping Your Promises

Children remember promises.

Every single one.

Even the small ones:

- ❖ "I'll play with you after dinner."
- ❖ "We'll read before bed."
- ❖ "I'll come to your game."

To children, promises are not casual statements — they are emotional commitments.

When you keep a promise, their trust deepens.

When you break a promise repeatedly, their trust weakens.

But here is the grace-filled truth:

You don't have to keep every promise — life happens.

Integrity is not perfection; it is repair.

A simple:

"Sweetheart, I'm sorry. I really wanted to keep that promise, and I couldn't. Thank you for being patient with me. I will make time for you tomorrow,"

goes a long, long way.

Repair is one of the most powerful integrity skills a parent can model.

REFLECTION: "Promises and Repair"

1. What promises do I tend to keep most consistently?

   Affection? Time? Routines?

2. Where do I sometimes over-promise or unintentionally under-deliver?

3. How comfortable am I with apologizing to my child when needed?

   Why?

Integrity Requires Boundaries You Stand Behind

Integrity in parenting means you don't set boundaries you won't uphold.

Children feel safer with:

- ❖ a few clear boundaries
- ❖ consistently enforced
- ❖ with calm follow-through

than with many boundaries applied randomly.

Children test limits because they want to know:

"Can I trust you to hold the line so I can feel safe?"

Your integrity creates that safety.

Even when:

- ❖ they push back

- they roll their eyes
- they pout
- they get loud
- they negotiate
- they test your patience

Your boundaries tell them:

"You are held. You are guided. You are safe."

Boundaries are not about control.

They are about love expressed through leadership.

Integrity Includes Honest Communication

Children can sense inconsistencies in what we say vs. how we behave. Integrity means:

- being honest about what you can and cannot do
- communicating expectations clearly
- not pretending everything is fine when it's not
- speaking truth without shaming
- offering explanations without over-explaining
- being age-appropriately transparent

When children see you practice honesty with yourself and with them, they learn:

- how to handle tough conversations
- how to tell the truth when embarrassed
- how to take responsibility

❖ how to communicate openly

Your transparency becomes their training ground for integrity.

REFLECTION: "Where Does My Integrity Shine?"

1. What part of integrity (consistency, honesty, follow-through, calm boundaries) is a strength for me?

2. What part feels hardest?

   Why?

3. What is one small integrity habit I can strengthen this week?

   (e.g., sticking to bedtime, lowering my tone, keeping one small promise each day)

Integrity Is Shaped in Your Imperfect Moments

Some of the most meaningful integrity lessons happen when:

   ❖ you raise your voice

   ❖ you get overwhelmed

   ❖ you react too quickly

   ❖ you say something you regret

   ❖ you break a promise

   ❖ you change your mind

   ❖ you feel exhausted or short-tempered

It is in these moments — the imperfect ones — that you have the opportunity to model humility, repair, and growth.

A simple:

"I'm sorry. I shouldn't have spoken to you that way. Mommy/Daddy is learning too,"

teaches your child:

- ❖ how to apologize
- ❖ how to take responsibility
- ❖ how to self-reflect
- ❖ how to repair relationships

Your child doesn't need a flawless parent.

They need a truthful one.

A growing one.

A grounded one.

A LIGHT-led one.

Integrity is not ruined by mistakes.

It is strengthened by honesty.

REFLECTION: "Grace for Myself"

1. What do I need to forgive myself for in my parenting journey?

2. What truth do I want to remind myself of when I feel I'm not doing enough?

3. How can I show myself compassion — the same way I offer it to my child?

Integrity Creates Long-Term Leadership in Your Children

Integrity today becomes:

- ❖ responsibility tomorrow
- ❖ honesty at school
- ❖ accountability in friendships
- ❖ good decision-making as adults
- ❖ courage to admit mistakes
- ❖ wisdom in relationships
- ❖ strength in temptation
- ❖ leadership in their future homes and workplaces

You are not just raising a child.
You are raising a future adult who will lead others one day.
Your integrity becomes their inheritance.
And even on days when you feel tired, stretched, or uncertain, your consistency, your honesty, your steadiness, and your repair are building something powerful in them.
You may not see the results right away…
but you are planting seeds that grow for a lifetime.
This is integrity.
This is leadership.
This is LIGHT.

CHAPTER FOUR

GOODNESS: Choosing Actions That Strengthen Your Home

The Power of Kindness, Service, and Daily Acts of Care

Goodness often goes unnoticed — but it is never unfelt.

Children may not always thank you for the meals you cook, the laundry you fold, the reminders you give, the prayers you pray, or the rides you provide. But they feel it. They are shaped by it.

Goodness makes a home feel safe, steady, and warm.

In the Lead the LIGHT Way™, Goodness is not just good intentions — it is good actions.

It is not just a soft heart — it is steady, loving hands.

It is not just "meaning well" — it is "showing well."

Goodness is the evidence of love.

It is love in motion.

It is leadership in action.

Goodness When Life Is Hard

Goodness is not only expressed in peaceful seasons.

Some of the deepest goodness shows up in the hardest ones.

Goodness shows up when you keep caring even when you're tired.

Goodness shows up when you keep showing up even when life feels heavy.

Goodness shows up when you choose kindness during stress, pressure, or exhaustion.

For many parents, goodness happens in the middle of:

- ❖ long workdays
- ❖ financial challenges
- ❖ raising multiple children with different needs
- ❖ caring for aging parents or supporting extended family
- ❖ doing the unseen, unthanked, everyday labor that holds the home together
- ❖ managing your own emotions while guiding your child's

Goodness in tough seasons is not small.

It is not overlooked.

It is not weakness.

It is strength in motion.

It is love under pressure.

It is leadership in the everyday stress of life.

Children may not notice the details… but they feel the effect.

They grow in the warmth you maintain, even in hardship.

They grow in the steadiness you model, even when stretched thin.

They grow in the calm you offer, even when the day has been long.

Goodness does not require perfect circumstances.

Goodness grows in the middle of real life.

Goodness Is the Helper's High at Home

Research shows that doing acts of kindness creates a natural "helper's high"—a boost of joy, connection, and emotional well-being for the giver.

But in parenting, this goes even deeper.

When you practice goodness daily:

- ❖ your home becomes more peaceful
- ❖ your children feel more secure
- ❖ your emotional patience increases
- ❖ your child learns compassion through observation
- ❖ your tone softens
- ❖ your connection deepens
- ❖ your child becomes more considerate

Goodness is not weakness.

Goodness is strength made visible.

And your children are learning — from your actions — how to become people of kindness in their own lives.

REFLECTION: "How Goodness Feels in My Home"

1. What simple acts of goodness do I already do every day?

   (e.g., preparing meals, listening, noticing their feelings, speaking kindly)

2. How do I feel emotionally when I show kindness to my child?

   Energized? Warm? Connected? Tired? Something else?

3. How does my child respond when I show extra patience or kindness?

Goodness Is Not About Being a Doormat

Goodness is not:

- ❖ allowing disrespect
- ❖ doing everything for your child
- ❖ saying yes all the time
- ❖ sacrificing your well-being
- ❖ excusing harmful behavior

❖ letting kids walk over your boundaries

Being good does not mean being used.

Being kind does not mean being permissive.

Being giving does not mean being depleted.

Goodness is balanced, healthy, and intentional.

Goodness is rooted in wisdom:

"I can serve you, but I will not enable you."

Goodness teaches boundaries with warmth.

It teaches responsibility with grace.

You are raising your child to be kind and capable —

not dependent, entitled, or unaware.

Goodness in Parenting Means Serving the Need, Not the Preference

Children often know what they want, but not always what they need.

Goodness means discerning the difference.

Sometimes goodness looks like:

❖ helping them with their homework

❖ giving them an extra hug

❖ praying with them at night

And sometimes goodness looks like:

❖ saying no with kindness

❖ making them complete a responsibility

❖   not rescuing them from natural consequences

❖   teaching them how to problem-solve

Goodness is not always comfortable —

but it is always constructive.

It shapes maturity, empathy, and emotional resilience.

REFLECTION: "My Goodness Balance"

1. Where do I lean too far toward comfort without responsibility?

2. Where might I lean too far toward responsibility without enough warmth?

3. What small change could create more balance this week?

Goodness Also Means Showing Tenderness in Tough Moments

Children grow emotionally through:

❖ gentle responses

❖ comforting touch

❖ soft eyes

❖ kind tone

❖ patient listening

❖ helping them name their emotions

❖ guiding them to calm, not shaming

Goodness is emotional generosity.

When your child cries, melts down, or becomes overwhelmed, your goodness says:

"I am here. You are safe. We will get through this together."

This teaches:

- ❖ emotional regulation
- ❖ trust
- ❖ safety
- ❖ connection
- ❖ empathy
- ❖ self-control

Children raised in emotionally good homes do not avoid problems—

they learn how to approach them with strength and compassion.

Goodness in Your Words Matters

Your words can nourish or deplete your child.

Goodness in speech sounds like:

- ❖ "I'm proud of you."
- ❖ "Try again, you can do this."
- ❖ "Your feelings matter."
- ❖ "Thank you for helping."
- ❖ "I'm here to listen."

❖ "Let's figure it out together."

Goodness also means avoiding:

❖ humiliation

❖ harsh criticism

❖ comparison

❖ name-calling

❖ shaming

A child's inner voice is formed by our outer voice.

Model goodness in speech, and your child learns how to speak kindly to themselves and others.

REFLECTION: "My Words at Home"

1. What positive phrases do I want to say more often?

2. Are there any words or tones I want to use less in my home?

3. What is one phrase I can practice this week that builds my child up?

Goodness Creates an Atmosphere Children Remember Forever

Goodness is what children remember when they grow up.

They may forget:

❖ the toys

❖ the school events

- ❖ the trendy moments
- ❖ the schedules

But they will remember:

- ❖ how you made them feel
- ❖ the tone of your home
- ❖ the laughter
- ❖ the warmth
- ❖ the safety
- ❖ the kindness
- ❖ the steadiness

Goodness becomes memory.

Memory becomes identity.

Identity becomes destiny.

You are shaping your child in ways you cannot see yet —
but the impact is already unfolding.

Goodness Prepares Your Child to Lead Others

When children witness goodness consistently, they grow
into:

- ❖ kind leaders
- ❖ empathetic friends
- ❖ responsible peers
- ❖ helpful siblings
- ❖ thoughtful spouses

❖ compassionate adults

You are planting the seeds of future leadership in the soil of today's goodness.

And just like a garden, goodness grows best when it is:

❖ watered daily

❖ tended regularly

❖ protected wisely

❖ nourished with intention

Your goodness today becomes your child's character tomorrow.

REFLECTION: "Goodness in Action"

1. What is one simple act of goodness I can do daily that strengthens my home?

2. What is one act of goodness I want to teach my child to practice?

3. How can our family make goodness a shared value — not just my responsibility?

A Final Thought: Goodness Is Your Daily Legacy

Goodness is leadership in its softest, strongest form.

It heals. It shapes. It anchors. It guides.

It says:

"I am here to help you grow, not just manage your behavior."

"I will serve you with love, not exhaustion."

"I will correct you with care, not shame."

"I will give when needed, and guide when necessary."

Goodness is the steady flow of love in motion.

It turns your home into a place where hearts grow strong, trust grows deep, and children grow confident.

This is not just parenting.

This is goodness on purpose.

This is goodness with strength.

This is goodness that transforms.

This is the LIGHT way.

CHAPTER FIVE

HUMILITY: Listening More, Serving Wisely, Leading Without Ego

The Power of a Gentle Spirit in Parenting Leadership

Humility sits at the heart of strong parenting. It is not weakness. It is not silence. It is not shrinking yourself.

Humility is strength wrapped in gentleness.

It is the ability to:

- ❖ listen without defensiveness,
- ❖ lead without ego,
- ❖ correct without pride,
- ❖ apologize without shame,
- ❖ and guide without needing to control every detail.

Humility is one of the most powerful leadership gifts you give your child.

Because children learn far more from the posture of your heart than the position of your authority.

A humble parent is steady, approachable, teachable, and safe.

Humility When You Feel You Must Be the Strong One

For many parents — especially single moms, single dads, or parents carrying the weight of the home on their own — humility can feel complicated.

When life is tough, it can feel like:

- ❖ you have to stay strong
- ❖ you can't let cracks show
- ❖ you can't admit mistakes
- ❖ you have to be the steady one
- ❖ you must look in control at all times

Not because you're prideful — but because you're responsible.

When you're the only one your child depends on, humility can feel like a risk.

But here's the truth:

Humility does not weaken your authority.

It strengthens your connection.

Humility does not mean:

- ❖ collapsing
- ❖ losing control
- ❖ giving up boundaries
- ❖ inviting disrespect

- ❖ "making your child your equal"

Humility simply means:

leading with honesty instead of pressure,

connection instead of tension,

and openness instead of exhaustion.

And parents who carry a lot often model the strongest humility:

- ❖ pausing even when overwhelmed
- ❖ listening even when tired
- ❖ apologizing even when exhausted
- ❖ choosing gentleness even under stress
- ❖ showing honesty without losing leadership

You don't have to look perfectly put together to lead your child well.

You just have to be real, grounded, and willing to grow.

Humility says:

"I am strong enough to be honest.

Safe enough to apologize.

Secure enough to listen.

And wise enough to learn."

This is leadership.

This is strength.

This is LIGHT-led humility.

Humility Begins With Listening More Than Speaking

Children need to be heard before they can be guided.

Humility listens to:

- ❖ their emotions
- ❖ their frustrations
- ❖ their fears
- ❖ their personalities
- ❖ their explanations
- ❖ their perspective
- ❖ their truth

Not because the child is always right, but because listening communicates:

"You matter. Your voice matters. Your feelings matter."

Children who feel heard are far more willing to listen in return.

Humility says:

"I want to understand before I correct.

I want to hear you before I teach you."

Listening brings calm into the home.

It lowers defensiveness.

It opens communication.

It strengthens trust.

Humility is leadership through listening.

REFLECTION: "How Well Do I Listen?"

1. When my child is emotional, do I tend to listen or jump into fixing? Why?
2. What is one way I could show better listening this week?
3. What makes it hard for me to slow down and hear my child sometimes?

Humility Admits Mistakes — Without Shame

One of the greatest gifts you give your child is allowing them to see you be human.

Humility says:

"I made a mistake. I'm sorry."

"I reacted too quickly."

"I shouldn't have spoken that way."

"I want to do better."

Some parents avoid apologizing because they fear it weakens their authority.

But in reality, apologizing strengthens your authority.

It shows:

❖ emotional maturity
❖ honesty
❖ responsibility
❖ self-awareness

- ❖ accountability
- ❖ courage

And your child learns how to:

- ❖ admit their own mistakes
- ❖ repair relationships
- ❖ calm their ego
- ❖ take responsibility
- ❖ own their choices

A humble parent raises a child who doesn't run from truth. Your apology becomes their blueprint for healthy relationships.

REFLECTION: "My Relationship With Apologies"

1. How easy or difficult is it for me to apologize to my child? Why?
2. What message do I want my child to receive when I say 'I'm sorry'?
3. What is one recent moment where humility could have softened the conflict?

Humility Serves the Needs, Not the Ego

Humility keeps parenting from becoming a battle of wills. Instead of thinking:

"I need to win this argument."

"I need to prove my point."

"I need to show who's in charge."

Humility asks:

"What does my child need right now?"

- ❖ Support?
- ❖ A boundary?
- ❖ A consequence?
- ❖ Comfort?
- ❖ A moment to breathe?
- ❖ Connection first?

Humility focuses on the needful thing, not the ego thing.

This helps parents avoid power struggles and shifts the focus
back to:

- ❖ growth
- ❖ development
- ❖ connection
- ❖ emotional stability
- ❖ wise leadership

Humility is not stepping back from authority —

it is stepping deeper into leadership.

Humility Shows Up in Tone, Not Just Words

You can say the right thing…

in a way that shuts your child down.

Humility softens:

- ❖ tone
- ❖ posture
- ❖ volume
- ❖ intensity
- ❖ delivery

It says:

"I am leading you, not overpowering you."

Children respond better to correction given with calm strength than to commands given with harshness.

Humility sets the emotional temperature of the home.

When you are calm, your home calms.

When you slow your voice, your home slows with you.

When you breathe before speaking, your child learns to breathe before reacting.

This is how humility heals the atmosphere.

REFLECTION: "My Tone and Posture"

1. How would my child describe my tone when I'm frustrated?
2. What tone do I want to be known for in my home?
3. What small shift in my voice or posture can I practice this week?

Humility Strengthens Connection, Not Control

Humility invites:

- ❖ conversation
- ❖ cooperation
- ❖ honesty
- ❖ openness
- ❖ emotional safety

Children follow humble leaders more willingly than forceful ones.

A humble parent communicates:

"I am strong enough to lead you, and gentle enough to walk with you."

Humility does not erase authority.

It enhances it.

Your child knows:

- ❖ you're not above them
- ❖ you're not against them
- ❖ you're not trying to overpower them
- ❖ you are leading with love

And that kind of leadership creates deep connection.

Humility Helps You Stay Curious Instead of Critical

Curiosity asks:

"Why is my child responding this way?

What is the root emotion?

What is happening developmentally?

What does this behavior communicate?"

Criticism says:

"You're too much."

"You're being dramatic."

"You should know better."

"You're always doing this."

Humility keeps you curious.

Curiosity keeps you compassionate.

This is how you preserve connection even when correcting behavior.

REFLECTION: "Curiosity Over Criticism"

1. When my child has a hard moment, do I usually respond with curiosity or criticism?

2. How could curiosity help me stay calmer in tough moments?

3. What is one phrase I can use to stay curious?

Examples: "Help me understand…" "What happened?" "Tell me more."

Humility Is the Cure for Parental Burnout

When you lead with ego:

- ❖ you feel pressure to be perfect
- ❖ you fear judgment
- ❖ you overfunction
- ❖ you take everything personally
- ❖ you carry guilt
- ❖ you expect yourself to know everything

Humility lets you breathe.

It reminds you:

"I don't have to be perfect. I just have to be present."

"I can grow while I lead."

"I can rest."

"I can ask for help."

"I can let go of unrealistic expectations."

Humility invites grace into your parenting.

Grace for yourself.

Grace for your child.

Grace for the journey.

REFLECTION: "Releasing the Pressure"

1. What expectation of myself do I need to release?
2. How can I show humility toward myself this week?
3. What kind of parent am I becoming when I allow myself to grow slowly and gently?

A Final Word: Humility Is the Soft Strength of a LIGHT Home

Humility is not loud or showy.

It is quiet, grounded, strong, and transformative.

It helps you:

- ❖ listen deeply
- ❖ love wisely
- ❖ lead gently
- ❖ correct with care
- ❖ stay emotionally steady
- ❖ connect authentically
- ❖ model maturity

Humility shapes children more than pressure ever could.

It teaches them:

- ❖ to apologize
- ❖ to admit mistakes
- ❖ to lead with compassion
- ❖ to serve others

- ❖   to handle conflict peacefully
- ❖   to communicate with honesty
- ❖   to remain teachable
- ❖   to grow without shame

When humility shows up in your home, emotional safety increases.

When emotional safety increases, behavior improves.

When behavior improves, connection deepens.

When connection deepens, leadership becomes natural.

Humility transforms parenting.

It transforms children.

It transforms families.

This is the LIGHT way.

CHAPTER SIX

TRANSPARENCY: Honest Communication That Builds Trust

Creating a Home Where Truth Flows Freely and Safely

Transparency is the LIGHT principle that strengthens the bond between parent and child like nothing else. It is the bridge between your heart and theirs. It is the foundation of trust, the source of connection, and the doorway to honest communication in your home.

Transparency does not mean telling your child everything.

It means telling them the right things, the real things, and the helpful things—in age-appropriate ways that build trust instead of confusion.

Transparency is:

❖ honesty without heaviness,

❖ truth without oversharing,

❖ clarity without anxiety,

❖ openness without burdening,

❖ communication without chaos.

It is the difference between hiding the ball… and holding space.

When a parent leads with transparency, they create a home where honesty feels safe, emotions feel welcome, and conversations are not things to fear—but things to grow from.

Transparency is not soft.

Transparency is strong.

It takes courage, self-awareness, and emotional discipline.

And your child will learn to trust your leadership because they trust your voice.

Transparency Begins With Emotional Honesty

Children learn to be transparent based on what they observe in you.

If they see you deny emotions, hide struggles, or pretend everything is fine when it isn't, they learn to internalize, mask, and shut down.

But if they see you say:

"I'm feeling overwhelmed, but I am okay,"

or

"I need a moment to breathe,"

or

"I'm feeling disappointed—I'll take a second and come back,"

they learn:

- ❖ emotional vocabulary,
- ❖ emotional regulation,
- ❖ emotional safety,
- ❖ and emotional truth.

Transparency teaches your child, "It's okay to feel. It's okay to name what's happening on the inside."

A child who grows up with emotional honesty becomes an adult who communicates clearly, loves deeply, and navigates conflict with maturity.

REFLECTION: "My Emotional Transparency"

1. How comfortable am I sharing calm, healthy truths about my emotions?
2. What emotions do I tend to hide from my child? Why?
3. What small way could I model more emotional honesty this week?

Transparency Does NOT Mean Oversharing

Transparency has wisdom.

It knows:

- ❖ what to say,
- ❖ when to say it,
- ❖ how much to say,
- ❖ and what to keep between adults.

Children do not need:

- ❖ the full weight of adult problems,
- ❖ the details of financial issues,
- ❖ the burdens of marital conflict,
- ❖ the stress of personal struggles,
- ❖ or the heaviness of things they aren't equipped to process.

Transparency is not dumping.

It is discerning.

You can be transparent without overwhelming your child.

For example:

- ❖ Instead of: "I'm stressed about bills,"

You can say: "I'm working on something important. Everything will be okay."

- ❖ Instead of: "Your father is getting on my nerves,"

You can say: "I need a moment to calm down before we talk."

- ❖ Instead of: "I'm so frustrated with life right now,"

You can say: "I'm feeling a little off today. But God is helping me, and I'm still here for you."

The goal is not secrecy.

It is safety.

Transparency without wisdom wounds.

Transparency with wisdom strengthens.

Transparency When Life Is Hard

For many parents — especially single parents, low-income families, or those navigating sudden financial hardship — transparency can feel impossible.

How do you stay honest…

when you feel like you must stay strong?

How do you build trust…

when the truth feels heavy?

How do you tell your child "We are okay"…

when you are not fully sure yet?

Here is the LIGHT Way:

Transparency is not sharing the full weight.

Transparency is sharing enough truth to keep trust safe.

You do not have to tell your child:

- ❖ "We're being evicted."
- ❖ "I can't pay the bills."
- ❖ "We don't have the money."
- ❖ "I'm scared of what's happening."

That is oversharing and transfers adult responsibilities to a child's heart.

But you can say:

- ❖ "We're making some changes right now, but we're going to get through this together."
- ❖ "Things are a little tough, but you are safe and I am handling it."
- ❖ "We may stay somewhere different for a little while, but I'm here and God is with us."
- ❖ "The lights are off for now, but it's being worked out. You don't have to worry."

This kind of transparency:

- ❖ gives clarity
- ❖ builds trust
- ❖ protects their heart
- ❖ honors their maturity level
- ❖ keeps communication open
- ❖ reassures them of safety

Children do not need the details.

They need the direction.

They need to know:

- ❖ "What is happening?"
- ❖ "Am I safe?"
- ❖ "Are we okay?"

- ❖ "Are you okay?"
- ❖ "What should I expect?"

Transparent parents offer truth with peace, not truth with panic.

This is transparency in the tough seasons:

honesty with stability, truth with tenderness, openness with protection.

And when your child sees you handle hard things with calm, grounded communication, they learn how to handle their own challenges later in life.

You are teaching resilience and emotional safety at the same time.

Transparency Builds Trust Through Clarity

Children thrive when they understand what is happening and why certain decisions are made.

They feel calmer when:

- ❖ rules are explained, not barked,
- ❖ consequences are connected to behavior,
- ❖ family changes are discussed early,
- ❖ expectations are clear,
- ❖ transitions are explained,
- ❖ truth is shared gently and timely.

This does not mean children get a vote in every decision.

But they do deserve clarity when those decisions affect them.

Transparency creates predictability.

Predictability creates safety.

REFLECTION: "Clarity in My Communication"

1. When I set boundaries, do I explain the 'why' or expect blind obedience?
2. How do my children respond when I give clear explanations?
3. What is one area where more clarity could reduce stress in our home?

Transparency Requires Showing Your Humanity

Children don't benefit from seeing a superhero parent.

They benefit from seeing a human parent who:

- ❖ tries,
- ❖ grows,
- ❖ apologizes,
- ❖ learns,
- ❖ admits mistakes,
- ❖ and keeps going.

Saying:

"I reacted too quickly."

"I misunderstood you."

"I could have handled that better."

"I'm learning too."

does not weaken your role—

it strengthens your influence.

It teaches your child:

- ❖ to admit when they're wrong,
- ❖ to repair relationships,
- ❖ to avoid blaming others,
- ❖ to develop humility,
- ❖ to remain teachable,
- ❖ and to take responsibility.

Transparency teaches authenticity.

And authenticity builds strong, emotionally healthy families.

Transparency Also Means Being Honest About Limits

Transparency says:

"I love you deeply, but I am not unlimited."

Children need to see you:

- ❖ rest,
- ❖ pause,
- ❖ ask for help,
- ❖ set boundaries,
- ❖ slow down,
- ❖ and take care of yourself.

When you communicate limits with calm transparency, your child learns:

- ❖ respect,
- ❖ empathy,
- ❖ boundaries,
- ❖ patience,
- ❖ and emotional maturity.

Saying:

"I need a few minutes of quiet,"

or

"I'm not upset with you; I just need to regroup,"

teaches them emotional responsibility.

REFLECTION: "Honesty About My Limits"

1. Do I communicate my limits calmly, or do I wait until I'm overwhelmed?
2. What limit do I need to communicate earlier or more clearly?
3. How might my child respond if I expressed limits with calm transparency?

Transparency Helps Your Child Trust Your Leadership

A transparent parent becomes a trusted parent.

Children learn:

- ❖ "I can tell them the truth."
- ❖ "They won't explode if I'm honest."
- ❖ "They want to hear my heart."
- ❖ "They won't shame me."
- ❖ "I can come to them when I'm struggling."

Transparency makes your relationship a refuge.

Your child will not fear your presence.

They will seek it.

Transparency is the heartbeat of connection.

Connection is the birthplace of influence.

Influence is the foundation of leadership.

This is how transparency transforms the home.

REFLECTION: "Truth in Our Home"

1. What atmosphere do I create when my child tells the truth—fear or safety?
2. What could I say more often to encourage honest conversations?
3. How can I become a parent my child feels comfortable talking to about anything?

A Final Word: Transparency Is a Lighthouse, Not a Spotlight

Transparency does not expose your child—it guides them.

It does not pressure them—it steadies them.

It does not shame them—it strengthens them.

It does not confuse them—it clarifies.

It does not overwhelm them—it supports.

It does not push them away—it pulls them closer.

You become a lighthouse.

Consistent.

Clear.

Warm.

Honest.

Grounded.

Steady.

Safe.

Your children learn:

- ❖ how to be truthful,
- ❖ how to communicate,
- ❖ how to handle conflict,
- ❖ how to approach people with honesty and grace,
- ❖ how to build healthy relationships,
- ❖ and how to lead with transparency in their own lives.

Transparency is LIGHT in its purest form.

It builds trust.

It strengthens connection.

It grows confidence.

It heals communication.

It transforms your home.

This is the LIGHT way.

And you are already walking in it.

PART TWO

Applying LIGHT to Real Parenting

CHAPTER SEVEN

Resetting Boundaries with Love and Confidence (Bonus Chapter)

How to Reclaim Leadership When a Child Has Been Given Too Much Freedom

Every parent eventually reaches a moment that sounds like this:

"I've let this go on too long…"

"How do I fix this without causing a meltdown?"

"Will my child adjust—or will this make things worse?"

First, take a breath.

You are not behind.

You are not failing.

You are leading.

And it is never too late to reset a boundary.

Boundaries in the home are not about control—they are about safety, clarity, emotional stability, and leadership. Children adjust far faster than parents expect, and when boundaries are reset with calm confidence, your child will feel more secure, not less.

THE LIGHT WAY™ 10–STEP BOUNDARY RESET PLAN

STEP 1 — Release the Guilt

Before you change any rule, shift your mindset:

"I wasn't failing. I'm learning. And now I'm leading."

Parents often keep loose boundaries because of exhaustion, fear of conflict, or wanting to show love. This is normal.

And now, you're choosing a healthier path.

Let the guilt go.

STEP 2 — Announce the New Boundary Clearly

Short. Calm. Confident.

Examples:

"Because you're growing, our rules are growing too."

"From now on, we will have a new schedule for _____."

"This change is for your safety and peace."

Your tone should sound like leadership—not frustration.

STEP 3 — Expect Pushback (and Stay Calm)

Pushback is not rebellion—it is adjustment.

Crying, bargaining, pouting, repeating questions, and meltdown moments are all normal reactions to change.

Your job: stay calm and steady.

STEP 4 — Repeat the Boundary Like a Script

Use CPR:

Calm. Predictable. Repeated.

Choose ONE steady sentence:

"The rule is the rule."

"The answer is no."

"Try something else."

"We're not negotiating that."

Do not debate or over-explain.

STEP 5 — Offer Two Positive Alternatives

Choices create cooperation and reduce power struggles.

"Book or coloring?"

"Room or living room?"

"Legos or drawing?"

"Screen off now—outside or puzzles?"

You are giving control within your leadership.

STEP 6 — Remove Temptation

Set your child up for success:

- ❖ Move the device out of reach
- ❖ Use timers
- ❖ Lock apps
- ❖ Create screen-free spaces

❖ Prepare the environment for the new expectation

This is support, not punishment.

STEP 7 — Hold the Line for 10–14 Days

This is the hardest phase—but the most important.

Children are asking with their behavior:

"Is this boundary real?"

"Will this change stick?"

Hold steady.

It becomes the new normal.

STEP 8 — Praise Cooperation

Reinforce their progress:

"You respected the rule. Great job!"

"I'm proud of how you handled that."

"Thank you for listening the first time."

Praise builds confidence and reduces resistance.

STEP 9 — Never Reopen the Boundary 'Just Once'

If you break the rule one time, your child learns:

"Ask enough and eventually it changes."

Consistency communicates leadership, love, and safety.

STEP 10 — Celebrate the Shift

After 10–14 days, acknowledge the change:

"Look how much calmer things feel."

"Thank you for respecting our new rule."

"I'm proud of how we handled this together."

Celebration closes the reset with connection.

THE THREE PHASES OF EVERY RESET

1. The Announcement

Short, simple, calm shift in leadership.

2. The Adjustment

Pushback, testing, negotiating, emotional release.

This is where MOST resets fail—but also where

transformation begins.

3. The Acceptance

Resistance fades.

Behavior stabilizes.

The home becomes calmer.

Most children adjust within two weeks.

HOW LIGHT PRINCIPLES GUIDE THE RESET

LOVE — Care + clarity = emotional safety.

INTEGRITY — Consistency creates trust.

GOODNESS — Protecting what strengthens your child.

HUMILITY — You grow while you lead.

TRANSPARENCY — Honest expectations, simple explanations.

You're not "being mean."

You're being a leader.

And your child will one day thank you for the boundaries you held.

CHAPTER EIGHT

Daily LIGHT Practices for the Home

Small Habits That Create Lasting Peace and Emotional Safety

Leadership in the home is not built through big, dramatic moments.

It grows in small, daily practices that communicate:

"I see you."

"You are safe."

"I'm leading with love, not pressure."

"We are growing together."

These simple LIGHT practices help your home stay emotionally connected, grounded, and peaceful.

LOVE — DAILY PRACTICES

Love is presence, tone, and gentle leadership.

- ❖ Give 10 minutes of undivided attention
- ❖ Speak one encouraging phrase
- ❖ Offer affection—hugs, gentle touch, warm eyes

- ❖ Hold one boundary with calm love
- ❖ Practice Compassion, Patience, Respect (C.P.R.)

Love is felt through presence and tone, not perfection.

INTEGRITY — DAILY PRACTICES

Integrity is consistency that creates emotional safety.

- ❖ Keep one small promise
- ❖ Maintain one predictable routine (bedtime, homework, meals)
- ❖ Model responsibility through your own actions
- ❖ Use calm, consistent follow-through
- ❖ Repeat expectations with patience, not pressure

Children trust leaders who are consistent.

GOODNESS — DAILY PRACTICES

Goodness is kindness in action—big or small.

- ❖ Do one act of kindness without being asked
- ❖ Use a gentle tone during correction
- ❖ Celebrate small wins
- ❖ Create micro-moments of warmth:
  - shared laughter
  - quick prayer
  - small treats
  - teamwork tasks

Goodness makes the home feel safe and calm.

HUMILITY — DAILY PRACTICES

Humility is soft strength that creates connection.

- ❖ Listen without interrupting
- ❖ Pause before responding
- ❖ Apologize when needed
- ❖ Ask curious questions:

"Help me understand…"

"What happened?"

"How did this make you feel?"

Humility opens the heart of the home.

TRANSPARENCY — DAILY PRACTICES

Transparency builds trust through honest communication.

- ❖ Share one calm truth about your feelings
- ❖ Name emotions without heaviness
- ❖ Communicate expectations clearly
- ❖ Offer reassurance when routines shift
- ❖ Be clear, not dramatic; honest, not overwhelming

Transparency helps your child feel safe coming to you with anything.

THE LIGHT CHECK-IN QUESTIONS

Ask yourself each evening:

- ❖ Did I speak with love?
- ❖ Was I consistent?
- ❖ Did I model goodness?
- ❖ Did I listen well?
- ❖ Was I clear and honest?

These small reflections bring awareness and growth.

A FINAL WORD ABOUT DAILY LIGHT LEADERSHIP

The goal is not to be perfect.

The goal is to be present, attentive, and intentional.

The more consistent these small practices become, the more your child grows in:

- ❖ confidence
- ❖ communication
- ❖ emotional regulation
- ❖ trust
- ❖ connection
- ❖ respect
- ❖ compassion

And the more peaceful your home becomes.

This is the LIGHT Way—

daily leadership that strengthens the heart of your home.

PART THREE

Growth and Reflection

CONCLUSION

Parenting the LIGHT Way: Growing as You Guide

Your Home. Your Leadership. Your Legacy.

As you reach the end of this Parent Edition, take a moment to breathe.

You have walked through Love, Integrity, Goodness, Humility, and Transparency — not as ideals to master but as practices to grow into.

LIGHT-led parenting is not about perfection.

It is about presence.

It is about growth.

It is about leading with intention and learning with grace.

Every chapter in this book points toward one truth:

You can grow while you guide.

You can lead while you learn.

You can reset while you rebuild.

Your child does not need flawless leadership — just faithful leadership.

They need a parent who is willing to look inward, slow down, and shine LIGHT in the everyday moments of life.

You Are Not Behind — You Are Becoming

Parents often feel:

- ❖ "I wish I had known this sooner."
- ❖ "I've already made too many mistakes."
- ❖ "I should have done better."
- ❖ "Why didn't anyone teach me this before?"

But the reality is this:

You are reading this now because now is the right time.

LIGHT was designed for your real life —

with busy schedules, imperfect days, rough moments, financial challenges, emotional stretches, and the need to begin again.

Parenting is full of new beginnings.

And every single day gives you another chance to shift the atmosphere of your home.

Where there once was tension,

you can bring calm.

Where there once was chaos,

you can bring clarity.

Where there once was inconsistency,

you can bring steadiness.

Where there once was silence,

you can bring connection.

And where there once was guilt or doubt,

you can bring compassion — for your child and for yourself.

You can start fresh at any moment.

That is the gift of LIGHT.

Your Child Will Grow From the LIGHT You Carry

Everything you are learning is shaping:

- ❖ how your child feels
- ❖ how they recover
- ❖ how they communicate
- ❖ how they trust
- ❖ how they make decisions
- ❖ how they handle challenges
- ❖ how they treat others
- ❖ how they see themselves

Even if they cannot articulate it yet.

Even if it feels slow.

Even if it doesn't look perfect.

Your LIGHT is forming something in them that will last.

One day, they will speak about:

- ❖ the safety you provided

- ❖ the love you demonstrated
- ❖ the truth you shared
- ❖ the boundaries you upheld
- ❖ the steadiness you modeled
- ❖ the humility you practiced
- ❖ the transparency you lived

These moments become their foundation —

the place they return to when life gets difficult.

You are shaping their emotional home.

You Are Leading With Universal Principles of Strength and Humanity

Every LIGHT principle reflects the values that strengthen families everywhere:

- ❖ LOVE that nurtures
- ❖ INTEGRITY that steadies
- ❖ GOODNESS that serves
- ❖ HUMILITY that listens
- ❖ TRANSPARENCY that builds trust

You are not just raising a child.

You are raising a future adult who will:

- ❖ make decisions
- ❖ build relationships
- ❖ lead families

- ❖ contribute to their community
- ❖ influence others

Your leadership today becomes their leadership tomorrow.

Your LIGHT is legacy work.

You Don't Have to Do This Alone

There will be days when:

- ❖ you feel overwhelmed
- ❖ old patterns return
- ❖ you react before responding
- ❖ boundaries get pushed
- ❖ exhaustion takes over
- ❖ life feels heavy and unfair

Pause.

Breathe.

Reset.

You can return to LIGHT at any time.

Lean on:

- ❖ supportive people
- ❖ wise community
- ❖ rest
- ❖ reflection
- ❖ learning
- ❖ small habits
- ❖ steady routines

You don't have to hold everything by yourself.

You don't have to solve every challenge in one day.

You don't have to be perfect to be powerful.

LIGHT is not a burden —

it is guidance.

A Closing Thought for Your Home

May your home be filled with:

Love that steadies,

Integrity that anchors,

Goodness that strengthens,

Humility that softens,

and Transparency that connects.

May your child feel safe in your presence

and confident in your guidance.

May your home be a place where truth is gentle,

mistakes are met with growth,

feelings are met with understanding,

and leadership is shared through example.

You are not just parenting —

you are leading the LIGHT way.

And your family will be better because of it.

QUICK SCRIPTS LIBRARY

Use these for any boundary, any day.

Announcement Script

"You're growing, and our rules are growing too.

From now on, _____ is no longer allowed."

Reason Script (One Sentence)

"I'm doing this to keep things healthy and safe."

Boundary Script

"This is the rule, and it will stay the rule."

Choice Script

"You can choose _____ or _____."

Pushback Script

"I love you, and the answer is no."

Reassurance Script

"It's okay to feel upset. You're safe. We'll adjust together."

Consistency Script (Tomorrow)
"Remember our new rule.
The answer is still no."

REFLECTION: RESETTING WITH GRACE
1. What boundary do I need to reset?
2. What guilt do I need to release?
3. What script will I use consistently?
4. What two alternatives can I offer?
5. Who am I becoming as a LIGHT-led parent?

30-Day LIGHT Parenting Journal

Growing in Love, Integrity, Goodness, Humility, and Transparency—One Day at a Time

Parenting change does not happen in one big moment.

It happens in quiet, daily shifts—

in the way you breathe before you respond,

the way you listen before you correct,

the way you connect before you lead.

This 30-Day LIGHT Parenting Journal is designed to help you grow in small, meaningful, and sustainable steps. Each day gives you a simple moment to pause, notice, and realign your parenting with the LIGHT principles:

LOVE — showing compassion with clarity

INTEGRITY — standing steady and consistent

GOODNESS — choosing actions that strengthen the home

HUMILITY — leading with gentleness instead of ego

TRANSPARENCY — communicating with truth and calm

This journal is not about being perfect.

It is about being present.

It is not about writing beautifully.

It is about reflecting honestly.

It is not about adding pressure.

It is about releasing it.

Whether your home is calm, busy, joyful, complicated, or going through a tough season, these daily reflections will help you:

- ❖ stay grounded
- ❖ lead with intention
- ❖ notice what's working
- ❖ strengthen connection
- ❖ celebrate progress
- ❖ reset when needed
- ❖ grow in confidence and clarity

Each day offers a short prompt to guide your thinking.

Some days will feel light.

Some may feel emotional.

All will help you become more centered and more connected as a parent.

You don't have to complete all 30 days perfectly or in order.

You can start, pause, restart, and move at your own pace.

The goal is not speed—

the goal is growth.

As you begin this journal, remember:

Every moment you reflect, you grow.

Every day you practice, you strengthen.

Every insight you gain, you shine LIGHT in your home.

Let this be your safe space to learn, breathe, reset, and rise as a LIGHT-led parent.

30-Day LIGHT Parenting Journal

Journal

A Guided Journey of Grace, Growth, and Connection

DAY 1 — LOVE

Timeless Principle: Love is felt most through presence and intention.

Reflection: How does my child know they are loved by me?

Practice: Give one extra moment of affection today.

Affirmation: Love leads my home with patience and care.

_____

_____

_____

_____

_____

_____

_____

_____

_____

_____

_____

_____

_____

_____

_____

_____

DAY 2 — INTEGRITY

Timeless Principle: Trust grows when words and actions match.

Reflection: What promise can I keep today, even if it's small?

Practice: Follow through on one commitment.

Affirmation: My consistency builds trust with my child.

_____

_____

_____

_____

_____

_____

_____

_____

_____

_____

_____

_____

_____

_____

DAY 3 — GOODNESS

Timeless Principle: Small acts of kindness have lasting impact.

Reflection: Where can I offer kindness without being asked?

Practice: Do one quiet act of goodness for your child.

Affirmation: My goodness strengthens our home.

_____

_____

_____

_____

_____

_____

_____

_____

_____

_____

_____

_____

_____

_____

DAY 4 — HUMILITY

Timeless Principle: Listening creates understanding.

Reflection: Where do I need to listen more today?

Practice: Ask your child one thoughtful question.

Affirmation: Humility makes space for connection.

_____

_____

_____

_____

_____

_____

_____

_____

_____

_____

_____

_____

_____

_____

DAY 5 — TRANSPARENCY

Timeless Principle: Truth spoken calmly strengthens trust.

Reflection: What calm truth can I share with my child today?

Practice: Be honest about one emotion.

Affirmation: My honesty strengthens our relationship.

DAY 6 — LOVE

Timeless Principle: Love balances warmth with guidance.

Reflection: How do I balance softness and clarity?

Practice: Give one boundary with calm love.

Affirmation: I can lead with care and clarity.

_____

_____

_____

_____

_____

_____

_____

_____

_____

_____

_____

_____

_____

_____

DAY 7 — INTEGRITY

Timeless Principle: Stability grows from consistency.

Reflection: What routine needs more consistency?

Practice: Hold one routine steady today.

Affirmation: Consistency is my quiet strength.

_____

_____

_____

_____

_____

_____

_____

_____

_____

_____

_____

_____

_____

_____

_____

_____

_____

DAY 8 — GOODNESS

Timeless Principle: Kindness is most powerful in difficult moments.

Reflection: How can I model kindness in a tough moment today?

Practice: Offer a gentle response when frustrated.

Affirmation: My tone teaches kindness.

_____

_____

_____

_____

_____

_____

_____

_____

_____

_____

_____

_____

_____

DAY 9 — HUMILITY

Timeless Principle: Growth begins with honest reflection.

Reflection: What mistake do I need to acknowledge?

Practice: Apologize gently if needed.

Affirmation: Humility keeps my home peaceful.

_____

_____

_____

_____

_____

_____

_____

_____

_____

_____

_____

_____

_____

_____

_____

_____

_____

DAY 10 — TRANSPARENCY

Timeless Principle: Clarity reduces confusion and anxiety.

Reflection: What expectation needs clearer communication?

Practice: Explain one rule or routine calmly.

Affirmation: Clarity creates safety.

_____

_____

_____

_____

_____

_____

_____

_____

_____

_____

_____

_____

_____

_____

_____

_____

DAY 11 — LOVE

Timeless Principle: Presence is one of the greatest forms of love.

Reflection: How can I be more emotionally present today?

Practice: Give 10 minutes of uninterrupted attention.

Affirmation: My presence is love.

_____

_____

_____

_____

_____

_____

_____

_____

_____

_____

_____

_____

_____

_____

_____

_____

_____

DAY 12 — INTEGRITY

Timeless Principle: Children learn responsibility by watching it modeled.

Reflection: How does my child learn responsibility by watching me?

Practice: Complete a small task without delay.

Affirmation: I lead by example.

_____

_____

_____

_____

_____

_____

_____

_____

_____

_____

_____

_____

_____

DAY 13 — GOODNESS

Timeless Principle: Kindness toward yourself supports kindness toward others.

Reflection: What is one area where I've been too hard on myself?

Practice: Offer yourself one act of kindness.

Affirmation: Goodness begins with me.

_____
_____
_____
_____
_____
_____
_____
_____
_____
_____
_____
_____
_____
_____

DAY 14 — HUMILITY

Timeless Principle: Understanding grows when we listen fully.

Reflection: Do I listen to understand or to correct?

Practice: Let your child finish their thought without interruption.

Affirmation: Humility helps me hear their heart.

_____

_____

_____

_____

_____

_____

_____

_____

_____

_____

_____

_____

_____

_____

DAY 15 — TRANSPARENCY

Timeless Principle: Honest insight opens doors to deeper connection.

Reflection: What calm truth would help my child today?

Practice: Share one gentle insight.

Affirmation: Honesty deepens our bond.

_____

_____

_____

_____

_____

_____

_____

_____

_____

_____

_____

_____

_____

_____

_____

DAY 16 — LOVE

Timeless Principle: Compassion strengthens confidence and connection.

Reflection: How can I show compassion today?

Practice: Respond softly during a moment of frustration.

Affirmation: Compassion strengthens my child's confidence.

_____

_____

_____

_____

_____

_____

_____

_____

_____

_____

_____

_____

_____

DAY 17 — INTEGRITY

Timeless Principle: Strength shows itself through steady follow-through.

Reflection: Where am I tempted to give in for convenience?

Practice: Hold one boundary even if uncomfortable.

Affirmation: My follow-through teaches strength.

_____

_____

_____

_____

_____

_____

_____

_____

_____

_____

_____

_____

_____

_____

_____

_____

DAY 18 — GOODNESS

Timeless Principle: Kindness grows deeper when practiced together.

Reflection: How can our family practice kindness together?

Practice: Do one shared "goodness task."

Affirmation: Our home grows in goodness daily.

_____

_____

_____

_____

_____

_____

_____

_____

_____

_____

_____

_____

_____

_____

DAY 19 — HUMILITY

Timeless Principle: Awareness creates emotional steadiness.

Reflection: What emotion do I need to slow down and notice?

Practice: Pause before reacting once today.

Affirmation: I lead with a calm and grounded heart.

_____

_____

_____

_____

_____

_____

_____

_____

_____

_____

_____

_____

_____

_____

_____

_____

DAY 20 — TRANSPARENCY

Timeless Principle: Clear expectations bring peace and predictability.

Reflection: How can I make one expectation clearer?

Practice: Restate one rule simply and calmly.

Affirmation: Clear truth brings peace.

_____

_____

_____

_____

_____

_____

_____

_____

_____

_____

_____

_____

_____

_____

_____

DAY 21 — LOVE

Timeless Principle: Real love meets the unique needs of the person receiving it.

Reflection: What does love look like for my child's personality?

Practice: Connect in their preferred love language.

Affirmation: I see and understand my child.

_____

_____

_____

_____

_____

_____

_____

_____

_____

_____

_____

_____

_____

_____

_____

DAY 22 — INTEGRITY

Timeless Principle: Growth requires discipline and self-honesty.

Reflection: Where do I need more discipline as a parent?

Practice: Do one thing you've been avoiding.

Affirmation: I grow in discipline, and my child grows through me.

_____

_____

_____

_____

_____

_____

_____

_____

_____

_____

_____

_____

_____

_____

DAY 23 — GOODNESS

Timeless Principle: Celebration nurtures joy and strengthens connection.

Reflection: When was the last time I celebrated my child?

Practice: Speak one specific word of praise.

Affirmation: My words plant seeds of goodness.

_____

_____

_____

_____

_____

_____

_____

_____

_____

_____

_____

_____

_____

_____

_____

_____

DAY 24 — HUMILITY

Timeless Principle: Strength includes knowing when to pause or ask for help.

Reflection: What pressure am I carrying that I can release?

Practice: Ask for help or take a brief rest.

Affirmation: I embrace help without shame.

_____

_____

_____

_____

_____

_____

_____

_____

_____

_____

_____

_____

_____

_____

_____

DAY 25 — TRANSPARENCY

Timeless Principle: Structure and clarity help children feel secure.

Reflection: Have I been clear about family routines lately?

Practice: Review one routine together.

Affirmation: Structure brings security.

_____

_____

_____

_____

_____

_____

_____

_____

_____

_____

_____

_____

_____

_____

_____

_____

DAY 26 — LOVE

Timeless Principle: Love restores connection after difficult moments.

Reflection: How can I reconnect emotionally after a hard moment?

Practice: Share a hug or laughter.

Affirmation: Love restores connection.

_____

_____

_____

_____

_____

_____

_____

_____

_____

_____

_____

_____

_____

_____

DAY 27 — INTEGRITY

Timeless Principle: Boundaries protect peace and emotional safety.

Reflection: What boundary matters most for our peace?

Practice: Reinforce that boundary today.

Affirmation: My integrity creates safety.

_____

_____

_____

_____

_____

_____

_____

_____

_____

_____

_____

_____

_____

_____

_____

DAY 28 — GOODNESS

Timeless Principle: Small gestures create warmth and belonging.

Reflection: How can I make our home feel warmer today?

Practice: Do one small "goodness gesture."

Affirmation: Goodness lives in the details.

_____

_____

_____

_____

_____

_____

_____

_____

_____

_____

_____

_____

_____

_____

_____

DAY 29 — HUMILITY

Timeless Principle: Parenting grows us just as much as it grows our children.

Reflection: What lesson is parenting teaching me right now?

Practice: Write it down and reflect.

Affirmation: I grow with grace.

_____

_____

_____

_____

_____

_____

_____

_____

_____

_____

_____

_____

_____

_____

DAY 30 — TRANSPARENCY

Timeless Principle: Honest encouragement builds lasting trust.

Reflection: What truth about myself do I want my child to know?

Practice: Share one honest, encouraging statement.

Affirmation: My transparency deepens our bond.

_____

_____

_____

_____

_____

_____

_____

_____

_____

_____

_____

_____

_____

30-Day Reflection Summary

- ❖   What changed in me this month?
- ❖   What changed in my child?
- ❖   What boundary became stronger?
- ❖   What moments brought joy?
- ❖   Which LIGHT practice do I want to continue weekly?

_____

_____

_____

_____

_____

_____

_____

_____

_____

_____

_____

_____

_____

ACKNOWLEDGMENTS

I want to express my deepest gratitude to everyone who encouraged, inspired, and supported the creation of this Parent Edition.

To the parents who shared their stories, struggles, and victories—you are the heart of this book.

To the church leaders and ministry teams who welcomed the LIGHT framework with open arms, thank you for seeing its value and helping me shape it for families.

To my children, who grew with me as I learned to lead with love, integrity, goodness, humility, and transparency—you have been my greatest teachers.

To my grandchildren, who call me Grandma Cookie—I pray that the legacy I leave, just as my mother left for me, will matter for generations to come.

And most of all, to God—who gave me this vision, this message, and this opportunity to serve families with LIGHT.

ABOUT THE AUTHOR

Beverly K. Girton, MBA
Creator of the LIGHT Leadership Framework
Founder & Principal Consultant, Leading the LIGHT Way™ HR, LLC

Beverly K. Girton is a leadership trainer, HR professional, and personal development educator whose work helps individuals lead with compassion, clarity, and character. She is the creator of the LIGHT Leadership Framework—Love, Integrity, Goodness, Humility, and Transparency—a practical and transformative model used by parents, churches, nonprofits, and organizations to build trust, strengthen communication, and cultivate healthy relationships.

As a mother of two adult children and proudly known as "Grandma Cookie," Beverly blends professional expertise with lived experience. Her insights are shaped by years of navigating parenting, leadership, ministry environments, and the evolving needs of families and workplaces. She understands the emotional complexity of raising children—balancing guidance with grace, structure with support, and leadership with love.

Through her writing, coaching, workshops, and leadership resources, Beverly equips people to bring the LIGHT principles into their homes, teams, and communities. Her approach is warm, practical, inclusive, and anchored in universal values that help human relationships thrive.

Her mission is simple:

to light the path and lighten the load for every leader—whether in the home, the workplace, or the world.

www.ingramcontent.com/pod-product-compliance
Lightning Source LLC
Chambersburg PA
CBHW041537120626
46551CB00019B/2730